WE GO ECO

THE CITIES WE LIVE IN

WRITTEN BY KATIE WOOLLEY

ILLUSTRATED BY SOPHIE FOSTER

WINDMILL BOOKS

Published in 2027 by Windmill Books,
an Imprint of Rosen Publishing
2544 Clinton St.
Buffalo, NY 14224

First published in Great Britain in 2023 by Hodder and Stoughton

Illustrators: Sophie Foster and Hannah Wood
Designer: Lisa Peacock
Series Editor: Melanie Palmer

Picture credits:
Esther Ruth Mbabazi/Reuters/Alamy: 29t.

Cataloging-in-Publication Data
Names: Woolley, Katie, author. | Foster, Sophie, illustrator.
Title: The cities we live in / by Katie Woolley, illustrated by Sophie Foster.
Description: Buffalo, NY : Windmill Books, an imprint of Rosen Publishing, 2027. |
Series: We go eco | Includes glossary and index.
Identifiers: ISBN 9781725398542 (pbk.) | ISBN 9781725398559 (library bound) | ISBN 9781725398566 (ebook)
Subjects: LCSH: Cities and towns--Juvenile literature. | Sustainable architecture--Juvenile literature. |
Smart cities--Juvenile literature.
Classification: LCC HT152.W66 2027 | DDC 307.76--dc23

Printed in China

CPSIA Compliance Information: Batch #QS27WM
For Further Information contact Rosen Publishing at 1-800-237-9932

CONTENTS

CITIES OF THE WORLD

There are cities all around the world.
The first cities were built about 5,500 years ago.

This is Ur, in modern Iraq. It was one of the first cities in the world.

In the 1700s CE, cities began to grow.
In the 1800s, in Europe and then the United States, cities started to change as more and more factories were built.

People moved from the countryside to the cities to look for work.

In the 1900s, cities began to spread out and up.

Tall buildings, called skyscrapers, were built.

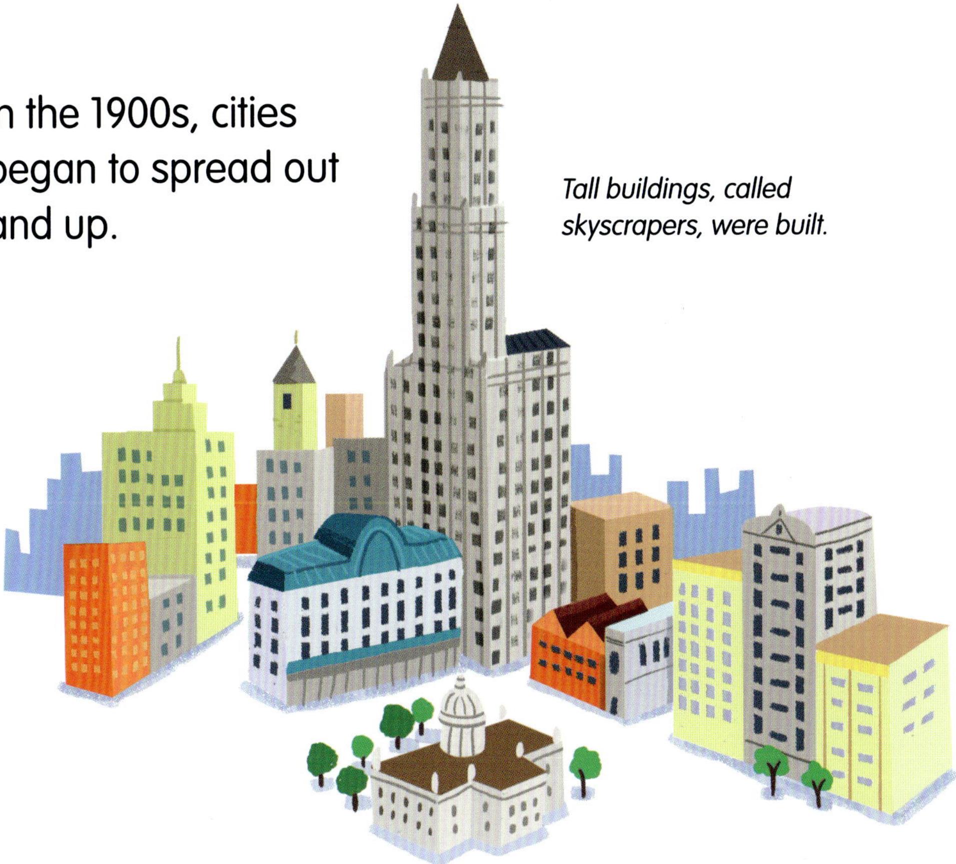

Today, big cities take up lots of space in countries all over the world.

CITY LIFE

Today, more than half of all the people in the world live in a city. More people now live in a city than in the countryside.

Cities offer people more jobs, schools, and activities.

But living in a city is expensive. For rich people, life in a city can be good. For poorer people, living in a city can be hard.

CITIES IN TROUBLE

Today, cities are in trouble. Earth is slowly getting hotter. This is called global warming. Global warming is causing climate change, which can impact cities with extreme weather.

Floods happen when heavy rain falls for a long period of time and has nowhere to go.

A hurricane is a big storm that starts out at sea but can impact cities on land.

A tornado starts on land, sometimes near a city. It brings very strong winds.

A tsunami is a big wave caused by an earthquake or volcano erupting under the sea. It can destroy coastal towns and cities.

A drought is a lack of rain over a long period of time. Droughts affect cities and the countryside.

A heat wave is a long period of very hot weather. This can cause wildfires that can get close to cities.

Cities today must cope with more extreme weather every year. But cities are also a part of the problem.

CITY POLLUTION

As more cities develop and as cities get bigger, more buildings are built, more people live there, and there are more vehicles on the roads. This means more pollution. Pollution plays a big part in climate change.

Pollution is what happens when harmful substances are added to the air, water, or land.

Smog is a kind of air pollution often found in citties. It is a mix of fog, smoke, and harmful gases.

CITY TRANSPORTATION

Air pollution and harmful gases in the air contribute to climate change. Air pollution in a city can also harm people's health.

Lots of cities must deal with air pollution and harmful gases from busy roads.

People in cities need to reduce air pollution. They can do this by walking, biking, or using public transportation instead of driving their cars.

In Hangzhou, China, people in the city hire bikes.

In Copenhagen, Denmark, a bicycle superhighway has made cycling safer.

ECO-TIP
When you are in a city, try to walk or use public transportation.

CITY ENERGY

Cities use most of the world's energy.
Energy makes things move and work.
Lots of people in lots of cities use lots of energy.

All the vehicles and buildings in a city use a lot of energy.

A lot of the energy used to power a city comes from nonrenewable energy sources, such as fossil fuels like coal, oil, or gas.

DIFFERENT TYPES OF ENERGY

Nonrenewable energy sources, such coal and oil, will run out one day. We need to use more renewable energy sources, such as solar and wind power. These are made from sources found naturally on the planet and do not run out.

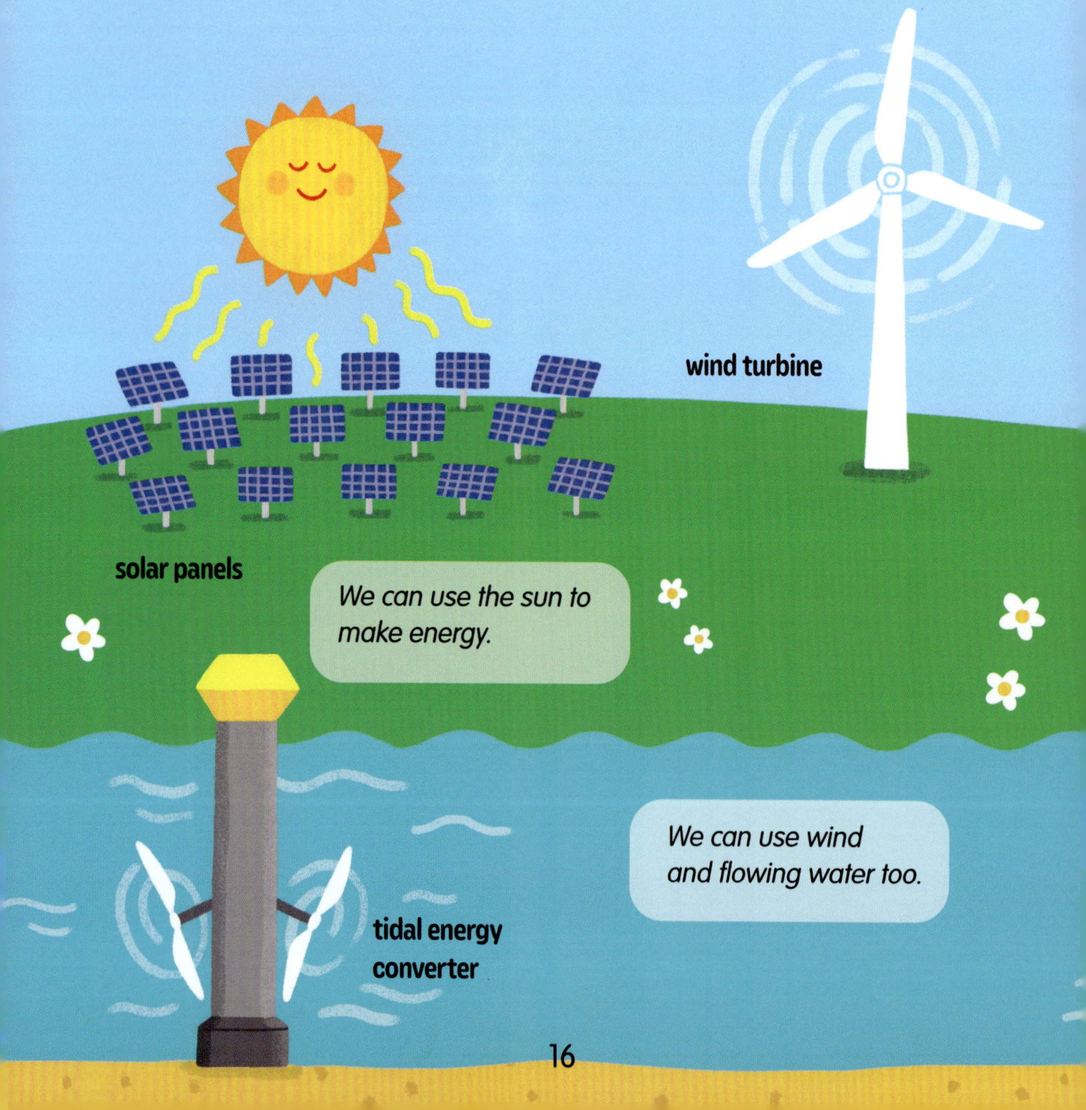

City leaders are looking at ways to use more renewable energy to power public transportation, such as buses and trains. Today, there are more electric vehicles on city roads too.

Shenzhen, China, has 16,000 electric buses with 40,000 charging stations!

GREEN CITIES

The good news is that there are things the people who run cities can do to help save the planet.

They can protect their green spaces. A park's trees and plants help keep the air clean.

Parks also give people a place to relax outside.

The people in a busy city make a lot of heat. This heat gets trapped, and people often use more energy to cool down. Plants and trees help keep cities cool. They provide shade and store less heat than buildings.

CITY HOMES

As cities get bigger, we need to build more homes, schools, and buildings. Here are some ways we can build new homes and offices that use less energy.

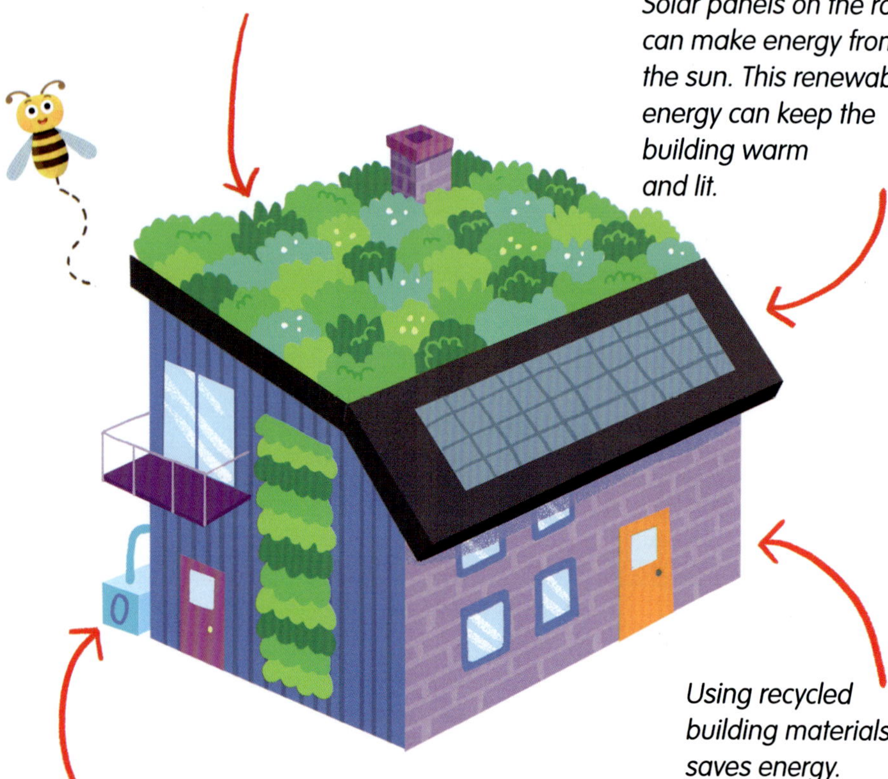

There are sometimes old buildings in cities too. How can we make them more energy efficient? One way is to insulate old buildings. This means using special materials to slow down the flow of heat in and out of a building.

Insulation helps keep the building warmer or cooler for longer.

ECO-TIP
Turn off the light when you are not in your bedroom. This will save energy too.

A CARBON FOOTPRINT

Every country, city, office, school, home, person, and action has a carbon footprint. A carbon footprint is the amount of carbon dioxide (a greenhouse gas) that is sent into the air because of energy use.

We can lower a city's carbon footprint by planting trees, walking or biking more, and using less nonrenewable energy.

Buildings, transportation, and the way we live in a city affect its carbon footprint.

ECO-TIP

What can you do to make your carbon footprint smaller?

A CITY COMMUNITY

City communities can find ways to help the planet.

In Rosario, Argentina, people can grow food on city land. This creates more green space in the city. The soil used to grow the food can also absorb water – reducing the risk of floods.

People can sell the food they grow at local markets and make money.

In Nairobi, Kenya, floods often destroy homes. People in the city are working together to rebuild public spaces with strong flood defenses.

These public spaces are safe places for everyone to live and work.

BECOME AN ECO WARRIOR

We can all help care for the planet. The people who run cities are beginning to make changes that will help Earth. But you don't have to live in a city to be a part of the change.

Set up an eco squad at your school. You could share ideas about how to make your carbon footprints smaller.

Share car trips with neighbors and friends in your community.

Grow your own food or help in a community garden. You could donate some of your produce to a food bank that helps people get the food they need.

Plan a day to pick up trash on your street.

Reuse materials to make other things at home.

Give your old clothes to other people who will wear them again.

EARTH ACTIVIST: VANESSA NAKATE

Vanessa grew up in Kampala, a large city in Uganda in Africa. Uganda is getting hotter because of climate change. Floods and landslides are harming it. People are losing their homes and their lives.

Vanessa saw this happening in her city. So, she set up Youth for Future Africa to speak out about climate change and its impact on Africa.

Vanessa wants us to speak out about climate change, its causes, and its effects.

GLOSSARY

Carbon footprint the amount of carbon dioxide released into the atmosphere as a result of the activities of a person, business, building, or community

Climate change long-term changes in Earth's temperature

Energy efficient used to describe things that use only as much energy as is needed, without wasting any

Expensive costing a lot of money

Extreme weather powerful weather that is not normal and can harm the planet

Flood defense a system put in place to reduce or stop damage by floodwater

Fossil fuel a fuel made from the remains of old life forms, such as oil, coal, and gas

Greenhouse gas one of the gases in Earth's atmosphere that traps heat

Harmful can hurt something

Nonrenewable energy an energy source that will run out

Pollution when gases, smoke, or other harmful materials are released into the air, water, or land, causing harm to people, plants, and animals

Public transportation buses, trains and other forms of transportation that are available to people to use, sometimes for a fee, and that run on fixed routes

Renewable energy an energy source that will not run out, such as wind or solar power

INDEX